ART

A
SCHZIOPHRENIC PERFORMANCE

B S

BHAMRA

Published in 2014 by FeedARead.com Publishing

Copyright © The author as named on the

book cover.

The author or authors assert their moral right under the Copyright, Designs and Patents Act, 1988, to be identified as the author or authors of this work.

All Rights reserved. No part of this publication may be reproduced, copied, stored in a retrieval system, or transmitted, in any form or by any means, without the prior written consent of the copyright holder, nor be otherwise circulated in any form of binding or cover other than that in which it is published and without a similar condition being imposed on the subsequent purchaser.

A CIP catalogue record for this title is available from the British Library.

The piece that I want to write about is called through the darkness. To me it is a drawing of peace.

you have to piece it together you may call it what you like. It is one of my smaller pieces. At the time

I was not sure what I was creating, what I was drawing or what I was feeling at the time the two colours black and white, sombre again the white calming, white I found powerful to use.

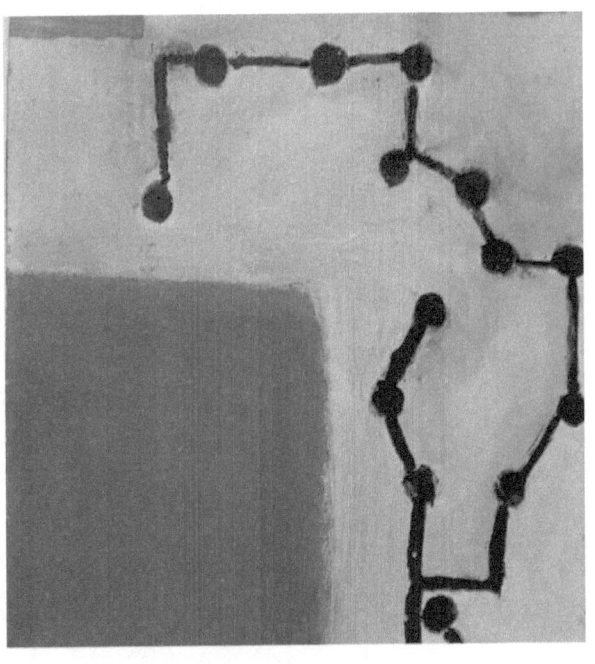

This piece was drawn and painted I think it is obvious that it states clearly that you are totally nuts it is the power of being the loner of my collection.

This is a beautiful drawing the way to draw I just drew it splashed it on actually at the time I was running out of ink and I was stuck with just one

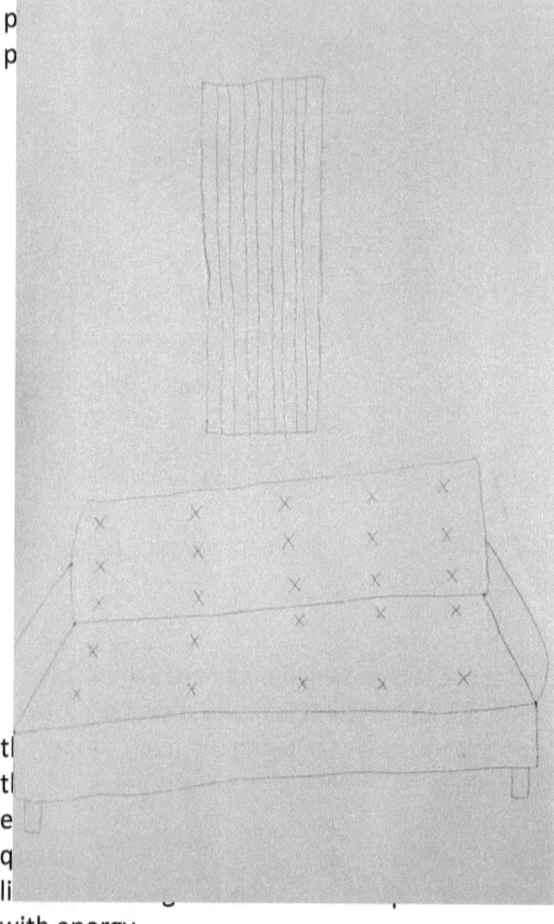

with energy.

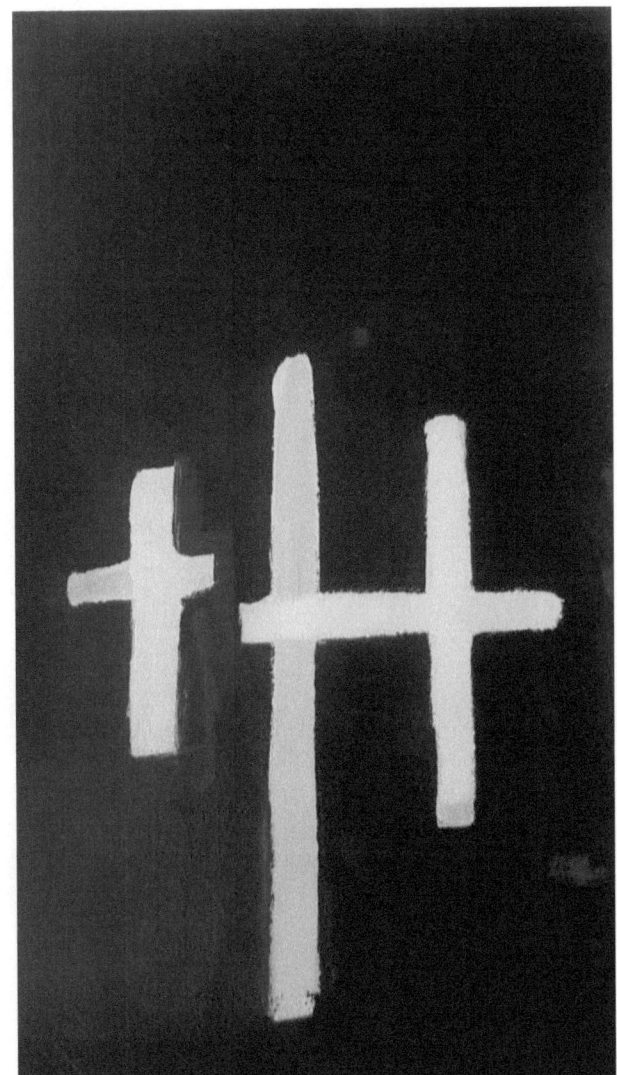

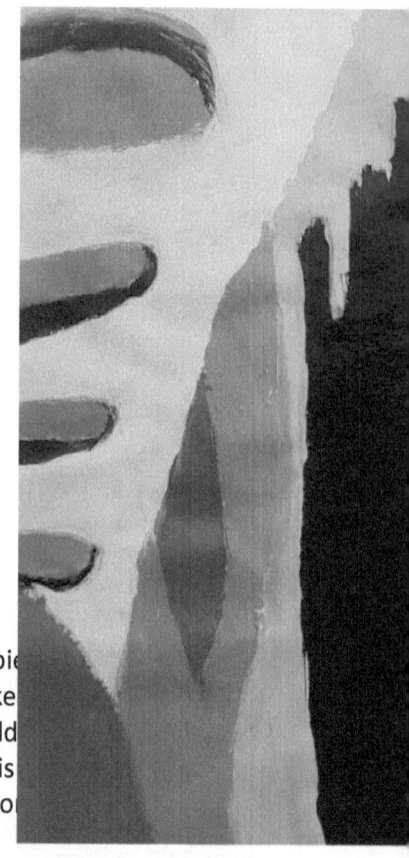

This piece is a simple pie
and a bridge it looks like
says what it says. I could
around this piece as it is
would normally draw so

This piece is an abstract piece some people say it is almost musical and flows with energy and look again you might change your mind. I could never get ny mind around how I created it. the question is who is behind the door.

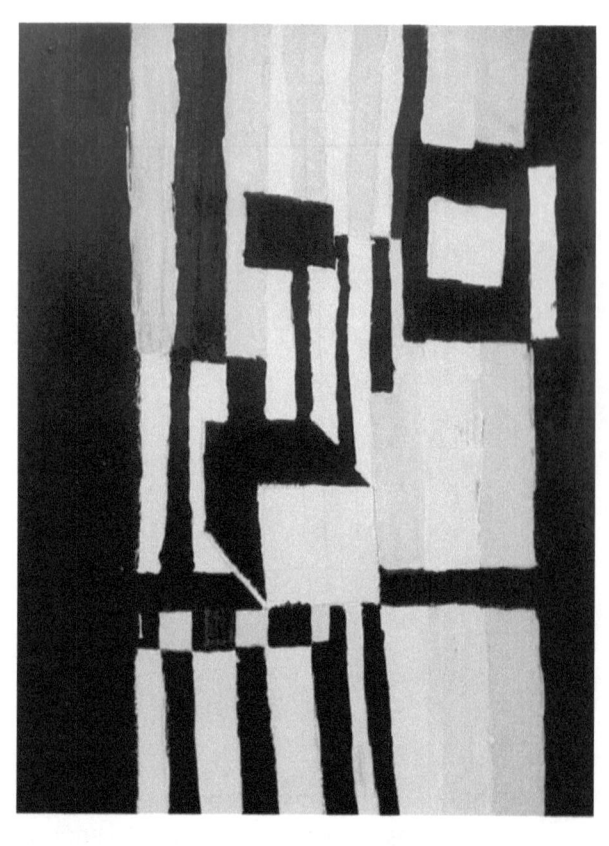

As for art it has been passion of mine since I was a teenager I started drawing abstract picture at school only to fail my A-level. And that for was a shock as I dropped out failing completely. The few months that I had spent at college were good the most that I did when I was their was slupter and to be honest in was not particularly good at that I created one more piece before I completely left the course. I had lost the passion for this subject completely.

However now have new ideas and with the technology it has helped although I like the old fashion way. I am not much of a drawer and I like things that are right filled with colour. I like design even though I have no knowledge of how to design and the fur that I have been would be a book cover. As for my art now it some people like it as I have maintained it within the last few years as I have got in to a bit more with a little encouragement.

The things that I enjoy are mainly abstract picture , for instants would take something that I may see in my home look at it and then think that it could be art and not only this I would put thing's together for example an old beer can then I would place a half used cigarette on top of it and there through my mind I would think that would be it and then what would it mean for instants you might see something totally different to me for example going back to the can and cigarette I would look at that and see a good side to it like somebody has been having a good time you may look at it and think the complete opposite I do not know what this is called but it seems to work the opposite though seeing something that is bad but is good or seeing something bad which is bad or again seeing something good which was good at the time.

I would encourage most people I know if I was asked that they should try drawing a picture it is a good thing to do as for me like I said before I am not much of a drawer in that aspect in fact I suppose that you could say that I abused my hand by not practicing enough and not really having that burst that passion for it. although I know I still know very little.

What I like most is the colours there are so many, in fact I think that there are to many and I personally do use enough colours that are available. I tend to stick to the darker colours in my style which is abstract, I think that the dark colours and the sombre colours work better for me, I enjoy dark places and I enjoy little light especially in the evening. Taking in to mind that bright and light colours can always change the mood. In my case they remind me of the morning. Going back to my style it is like I am freed by the way I move my brushes, I like to feel the paint, I like to be able to move the paint around. Not really knowing the way it is going to move not knowing is the good bit. As it is a surprise I like to use the paint and lots of it not caring at the time, I watch my own movements and I always know that it never comes out the way I expect it to do, it is always different to what I try and visualized. I think with my kind of style it works for me and I enjoy having that gift.

I like my pieces reasonably small in size, as you have to really look to see the pictures to see them. With a large surrounding areas, I suppose you might think that it is large use of the space, as it would be a waist. Some people I think like there art big I suppose it depends on the size of your walls. Things being smaller it is just as powerful as having a large piece small can be powerful too, if that is what you see some times large is a bit over powering especially with the sombre dark colours. I like the primary colours the reds both dark and light and blue it reminds of the sky, the cowardly yellow and the girl pulling green and of course black and white.

As for what I draw and then paint which is my style, for this moment I have I do not think that I have ever painted a picture that I did not draw it a little first, as my drawing skills are not the greatest.

The subjects that I enjoy drawing are abstract pictures of hill sides and lakes with music and madness, I like cells the things that house the human body.

As an artist I tend to like the poorer things like rubbish and old things and broken things a lot of this subject can be found, dirty things like half smoked cigarettes and used beer cans. To find this style I had to become this person I was looking at it everyday watching the room change watching my habit change it was mind destroying I could see the whole thing revolving and I waited for the very last second to capture the pictures that i wanted to express myself in that way I would not advise anybody to attempt it unless they had a nursing team about them.

What do you visualize that is a good question, going back in my mind I have darkness no light the things that I see around me often are sombre. I think of life but my two subjects here seem to rebound off each other, I do not want to die except if you look to the future were else can we go. that is the darkness that I am talking about however there's is the light and is filled with life, what I have here are two opposites, confused I am.

To me it is funny how art actually works the moods and the enjoyment, and sadness that it can bring. I hope that not all of my work and it is not over yet makes somebody feel good, happy and maybe just a tear not that I want to upset you emotion plays a big part in my work especially when it comes to painting. As I am mostly dragged out of bed or dragged away from a tv programme or even more so to go out like I had forgotten something or I had be called away.

As for how my emotions works I find people interesting, I do not think that I have drawn many but in saying that the closet body that I have drawn would be a fashion doll. I can not draw people yet. Faces and expression I have tried and mine are always abstract, I think that the face expresses the most emotions not for the simple fact that is were tears come from the eyes. They play a really big part of our lives.

In my eyes art is everywhere inside, outside it is everywhere we look, if you look closely enough I suppose it could change the way you think even change your world and to have that creative ability is a real gift it is a incredible feeling that you have created something from your mind, your eyes, it is extremely addictive, question can you visualize to create and create. Once you have practiced it becomes easier and easier and better and better. Patence is a really good thing to have I do not have any my self I am all ways in a rush to finish what I have started, do not listen to me take your time as you are developing a skill I think then it will truly come.

This piece is expected to look like what it actually is I did not know what I painted until the end this is not what I expected when I look at it, this reminds me of apartment blocks. I do not know how I painted it is a summer piece.

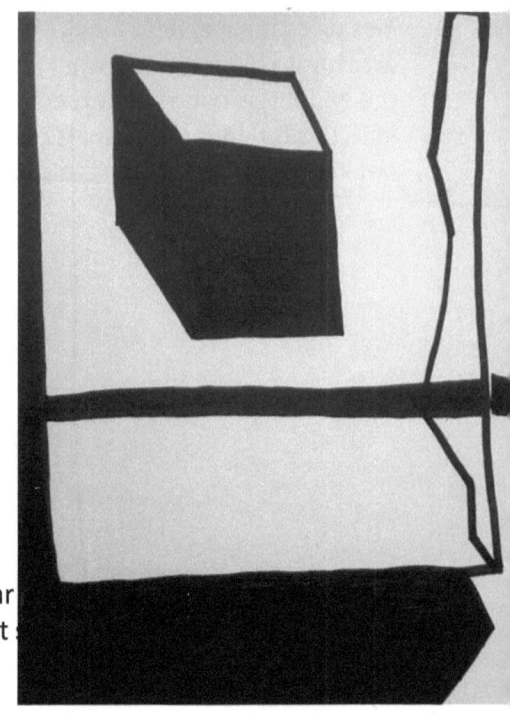

This particular
my favorites it
striking.

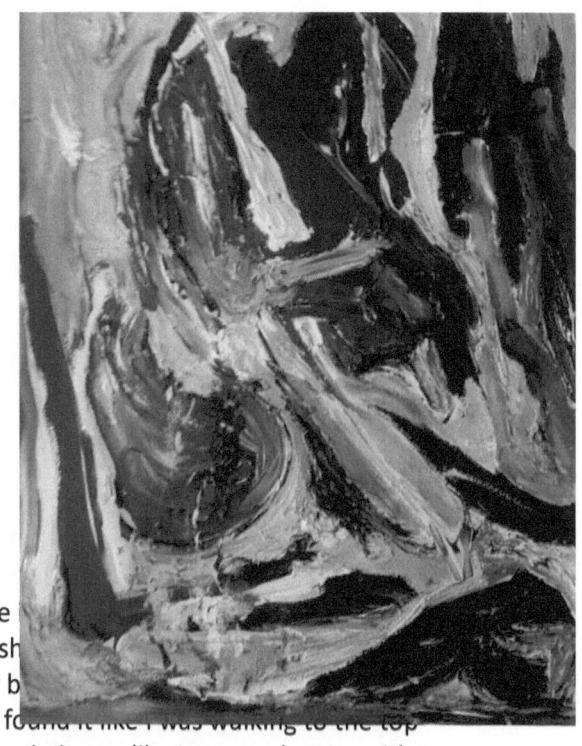

This piece shows pash character b the sun. I fo of a mountain it was like I was at the top with one more step before I reached the very top of the giant mountain.

As for my art part of it is design there has to be a balance for what I want you to see I do not think that any two people would see the exact same but might if prompted.

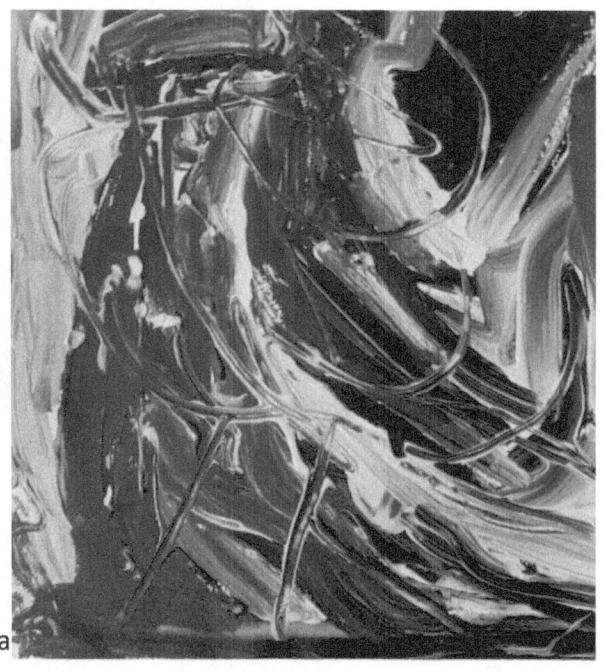

This is a

painting this particular piece as it draws you right in the lines as you look at them are drawing you in with a mixture of colour. Yellow and blue and the sombre dark black.

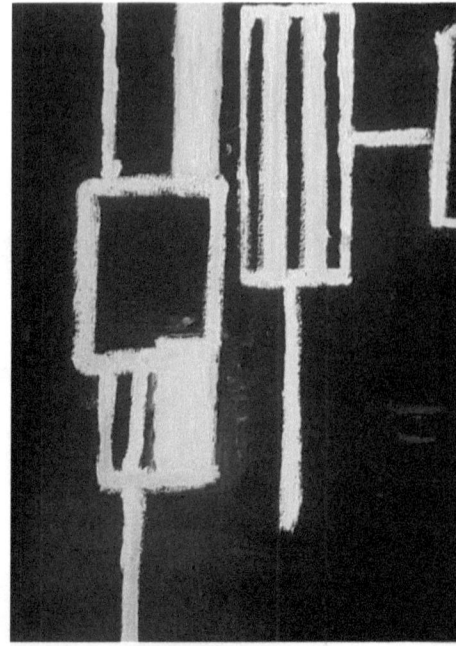

This piece is a simple it is basically what you see for some strange reason I think that it is a group of radio speakers yet when I look at it again it says to me prison, the colours black and white very dark.

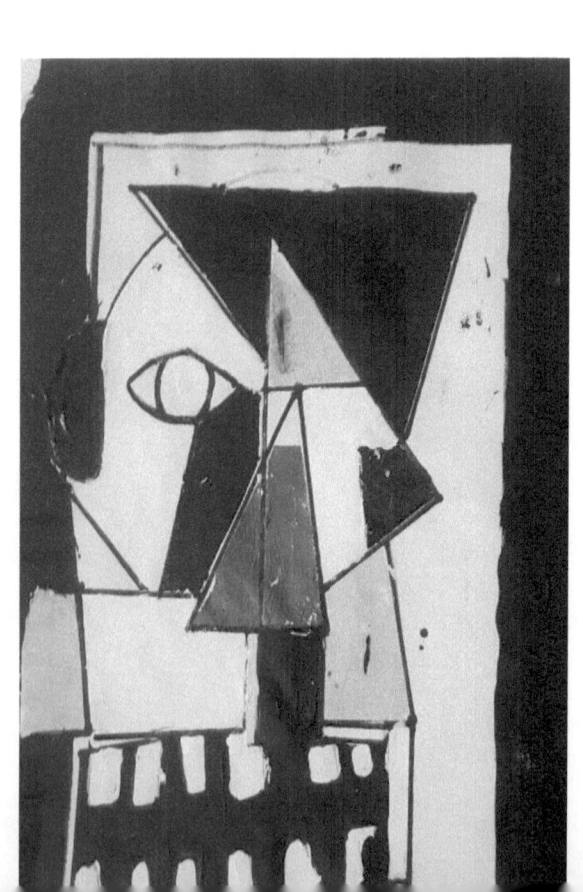

This is a self portrait of my angry self do not turn the lights off it is filled with all kinds of shapes especially triangles boy do I look u

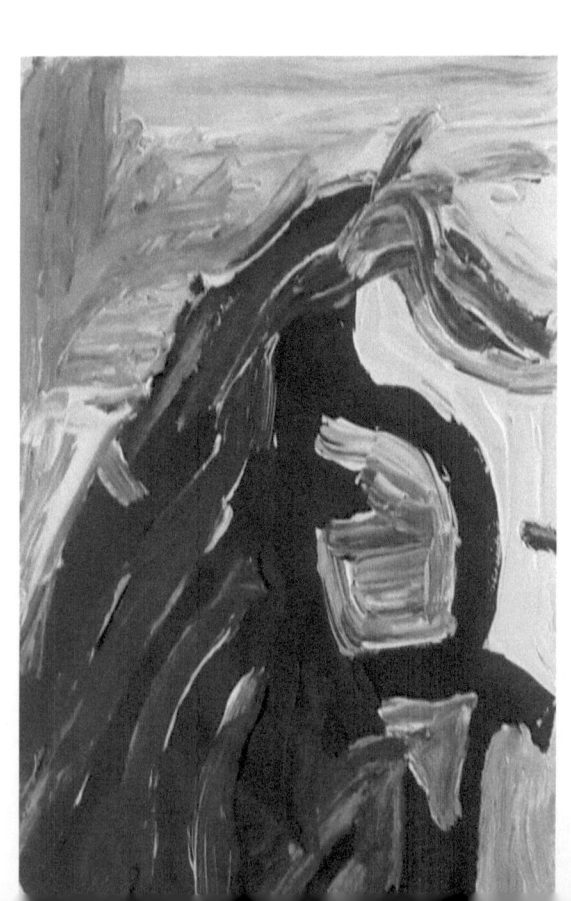

This piece is an abstract painting it has the way I was feeling at the point of what I was trying to achieve at that time it is a winter piece and it is cold piece.

This piece reminds of NEW YORK from the above looking down upon the building's the cold blue and the dark black it works four ways upside down the right way up vertical side ways
left
and
right
.

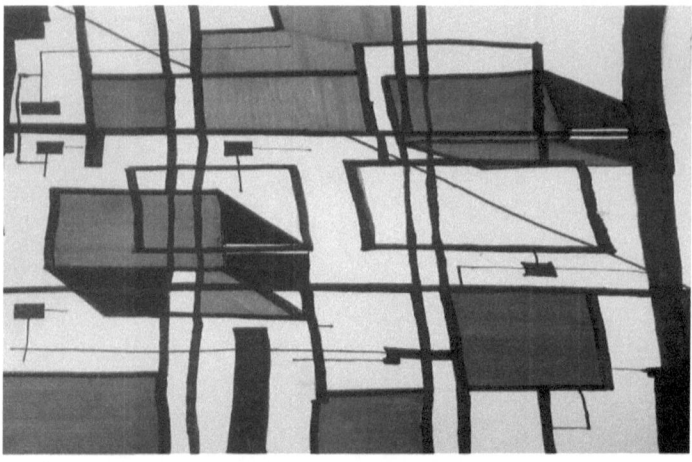

This is a abstract piece filled with frustration I sure that I was on a mad one when I painted this dark around it's sides with a burst of energy flattering the centre of the painting.

This piece is one of the most relaxed paintings that I painted in fact I do not know what it is to this day it started off as a set of squares on top of each other then all of a sudden it changed to this, it works on its side up side down.

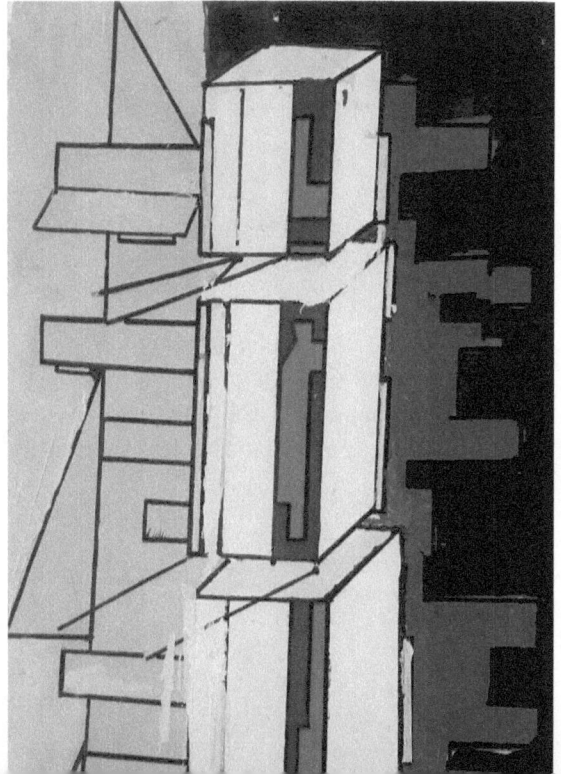

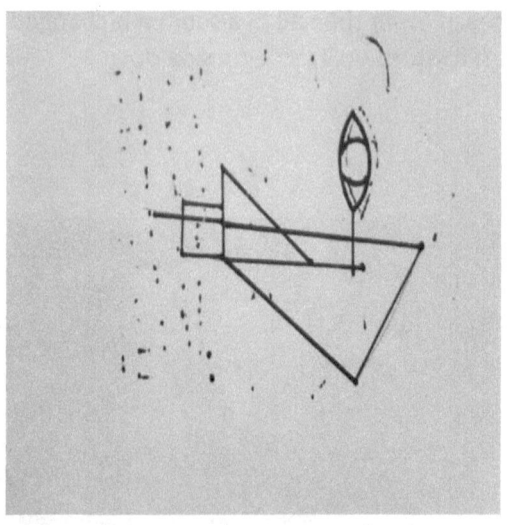

This piece is again a simple drawing it is basically another drawing of my face it is a sharp reflection I would like to actually make a sculpture of this particular one. It is so basic it looks pure and I think it

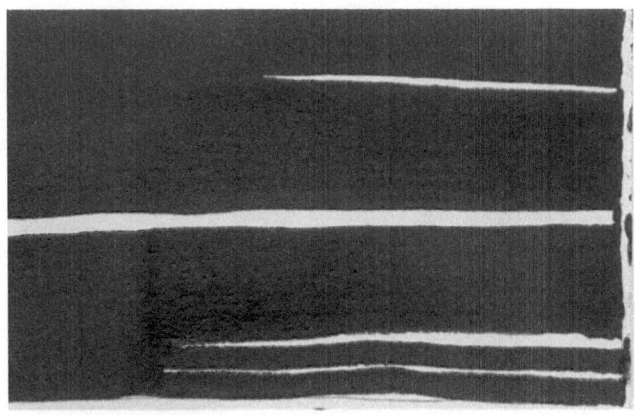

This picture is dark and light it works both ways and if you look at closely it looks like a small set of steps it is as simple as that.

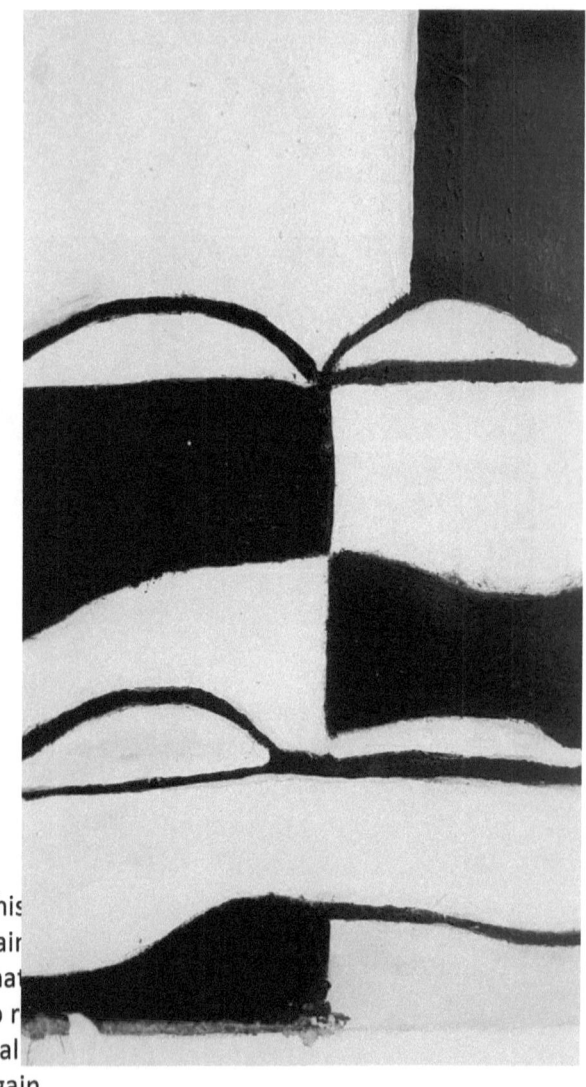

This
pair
that
to r
wal
again.

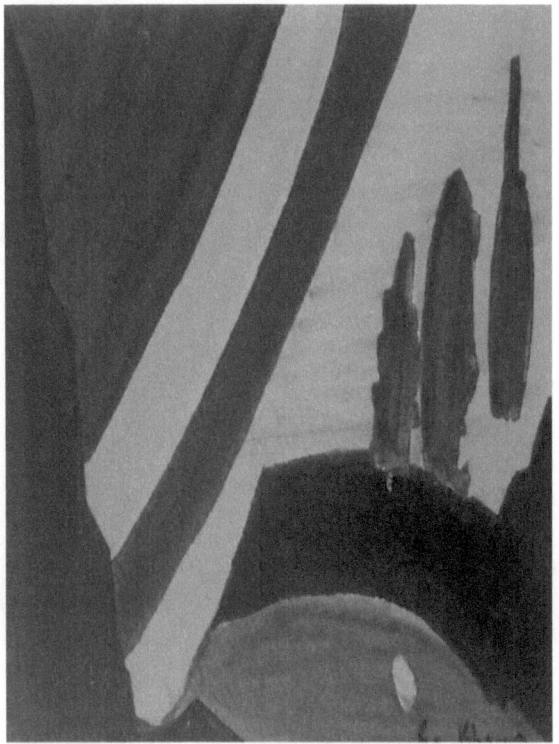

The piece in front of you is very similar to my bridge it is a very bright horizon in fact.

This piece is the awkwa[rd]
decide what I actually w[ant]
an abstract piece call it
the painting that I have
tempted to destroy it. I[t]
boo for some reason.

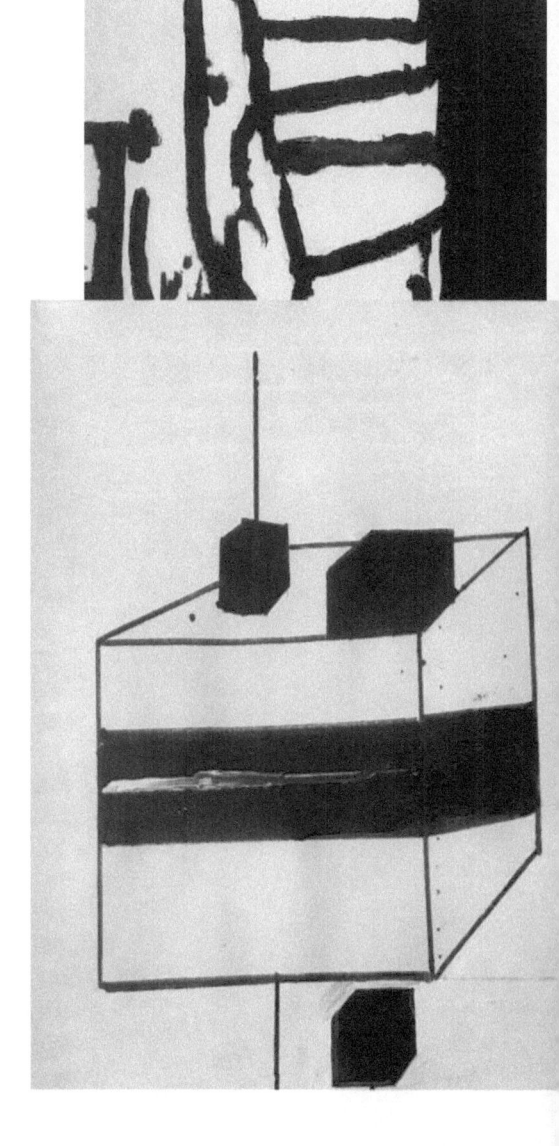

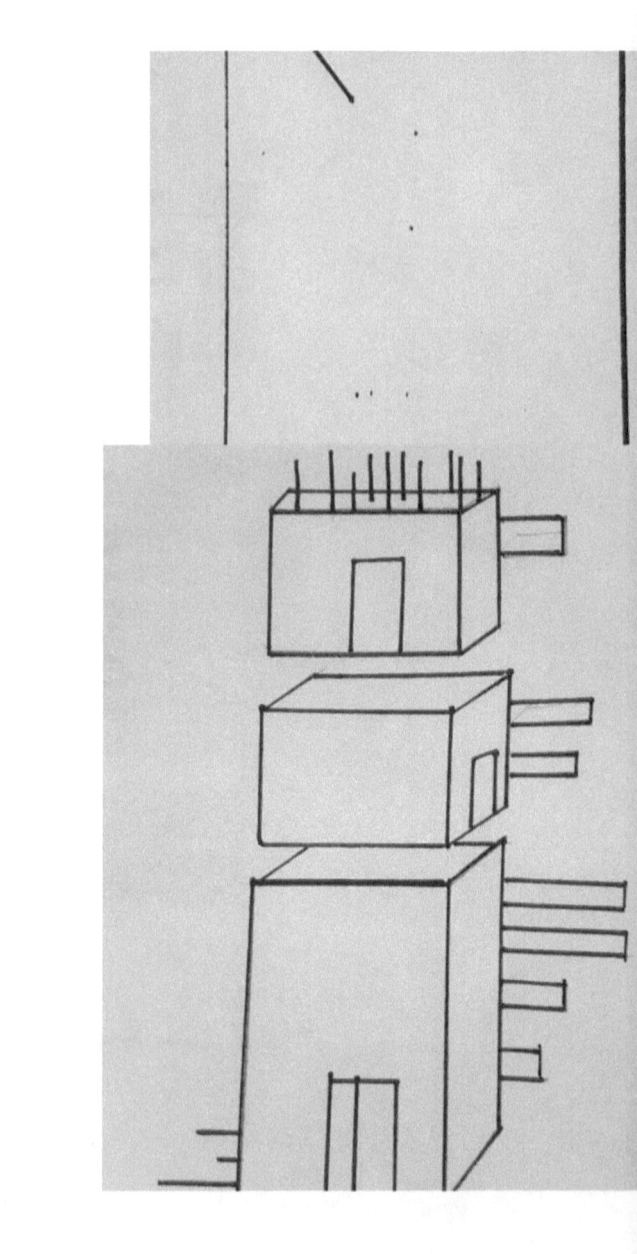

These four picture above I will start with the third lets do it in reverse the third the picture that you see in front you is basically a house that has part of it hovering then the second part is hovering too and the third part is the same. The picture itself is in black marker it grows on you every time you see it. with it's white back ground and the white building's itself. I think that I have fallen in love with this piece. This piece is so basic but I have put the thought in to my mind it straight forwards its and because it is simple it works. Sometimes the simplest things are better. The second piece I am not so sure as for the last time I spoke of the mistakes in the picture that I have picked for you I am not very fond of this one I will leave it at that. The last picture that I am going to tell you about in this short paragraph is one that I just about explain it is a dark picture it has everything grewsome and dark about it the stair case the only thing that is missing is the mice it is a crooked staircase. In black and white. The three picture s below are basically a little bit more scientific there are lots of lines and a few numbers in evolved as I will continue the first picture of the group of four is a drawing that seems to me to say science lots of squares the picture have no names it is as sweat as honey and there are things lurking around it more line s that look like mistakes.

Again another picture but this time half done why because the equation was only half done leaving the picture unfinished drawn in black and white it was simple to create but quite difficult to remove from my mind that's one of the reasons that I like it. Again I have chosen the simple shape of the square except this time they are in tangled and again it forces the thought of having the idea that there's is something mathematical going on but in reality there's is no connection and they are just squares. The last picture in this selection it is the last but one and again it has that science and mathematical look about it H20 water is life.

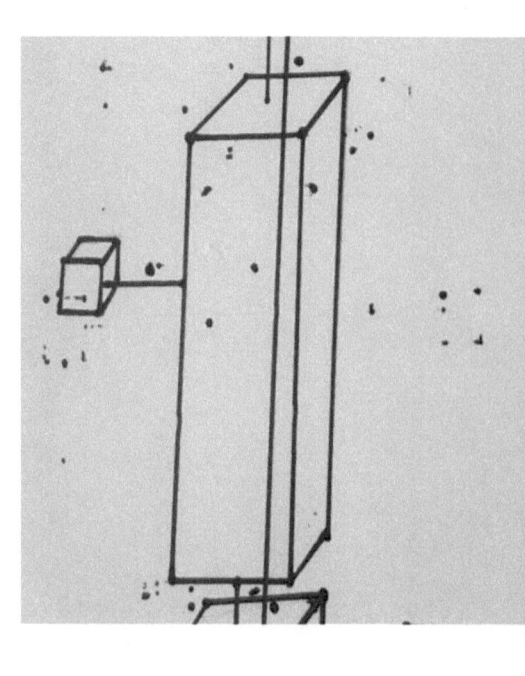

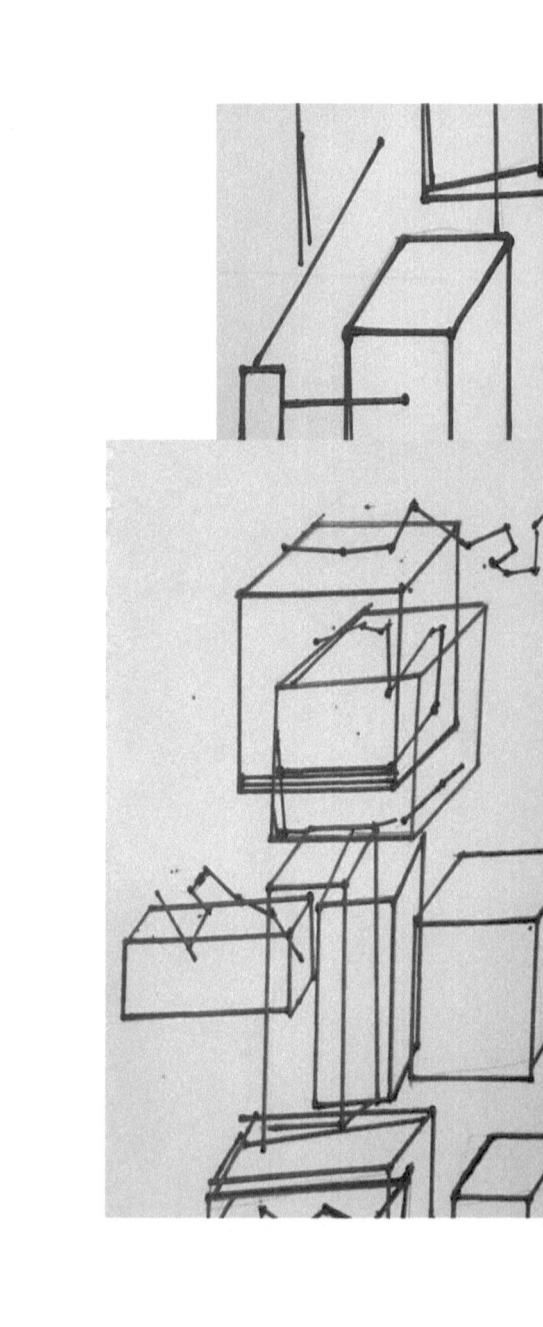

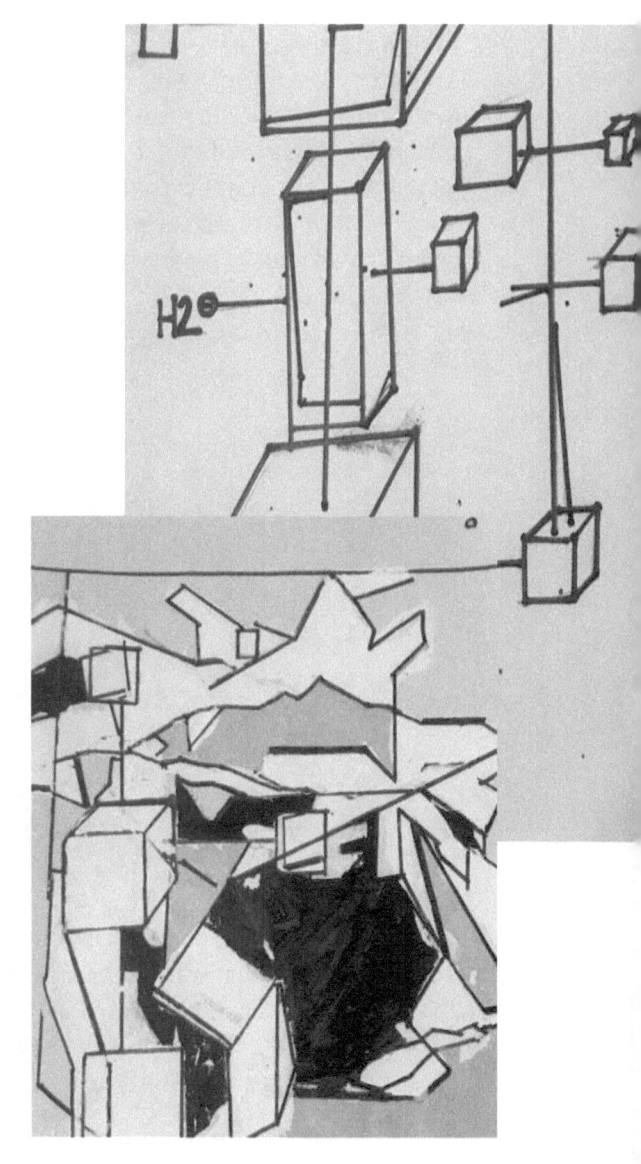

This picture was really good fun to paint it started of as a complete mess as I continued I was bringing it back to life with every stroke it was not until the end that it really became one of my paintings bright orange and yellow finishing it off with a black marker adding lines what I have actually painted I do not no it could be A MONSTER.

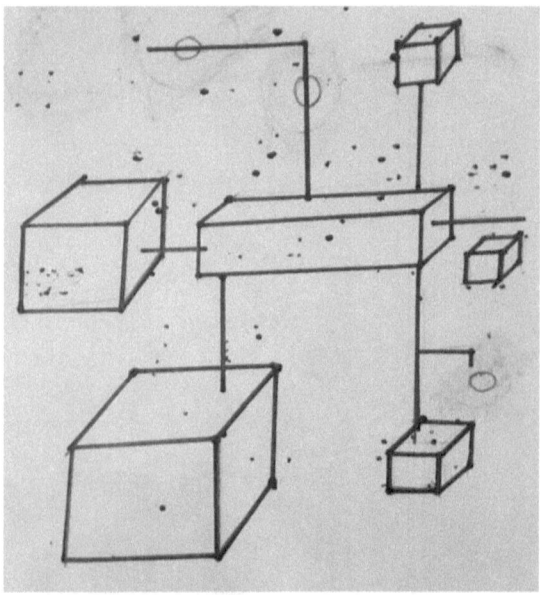

This is the last of five designs cross art pictures that I have created it was pretty simple as the marker just flowed as I drew it. It started with a square then rest collided a rush of energy bigger lines bigger shapes.

The picture below is just as it says it is half a rectangle cube going through half a square a simple design looks good up right too.

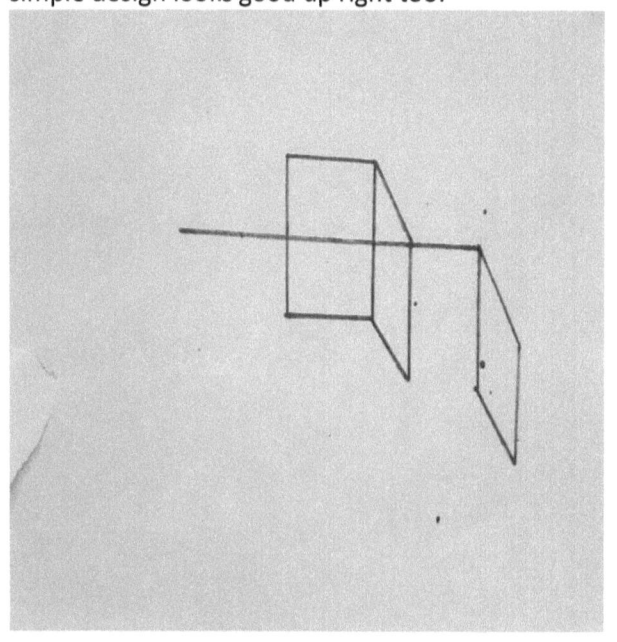

The picture above is clearly a vision it is made in the same way as the others there are four different pictures this is the third and below is the fourth it is dark and cold like a grave stone with knowledge its almost like looking at the winter sky's at night or even just night tiThis is one of four and really states that the night time is better than the morning again its darkness slowly out whiting you and sucking you into the dark ness of the actually drawing

This picture is a really bright and loving every stroke that I laid on the paper was a complete pleasure as it was one of the first painting s that I did I gave it three different names in the end I just called it Africa, before that it was called a sun rise and before that it was called mud hut.

The starving hand of the old person looking for some thing easy to cook and the only thing in the pantry is an old already opened can of baked beans.

This abstract piece is the third of four similar colours different thought it to me is a sun rise, sunset but in total darkness

This one is similar to a couple, again I could totally tell my self off as it was not that I did not put the effort in it just did not come out the way that I expected you know what they say. It is almost like the sea with an awkward beech it is a total mess I think. What do you think.

This piece is a magical piece the door in the tree it was definatly something that I will try and draw again the light orange sun setting changing to red close to pink the brown trees with no leaf's in and of course the door.

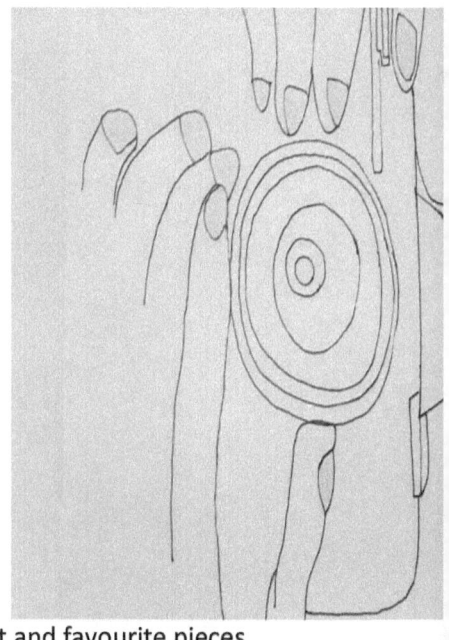

This is one of my very best and favourite pieces the camera I drew this a few years ago it says what you see the camera. It is in ink. The camera it says exactly what it does smile I'll take your photograph. The shape of the hand.

The picture below is basic a simple design squares up on squares. This is a fascinating piece for me and it was when I created it. I see a few things I look at this particular piece one a door and a long cave it works horizontally it is like a tunnel.

Land scape a beautiful piece but it has a beautiful wicked feel to it who is at the bottom I think that it is a brilliant attempt for a land scape in white and black all most if it was on the other side of the world or if it was on

The piece that I want to write about is called through the darkness. To me it is a drawing of peace you have to piece it together you may call it what you like. It is one of my smaller pieces. At the time

I was not sure what I was creating, what I was drawing or what I was feeling at the time the two colours black and white, sombre again the white calming, white I found powerful to use.

This piece was drawn and painted I think it is obvious that it states clearly that you are totally nuts it is the power of being the loner of my collection.

This is a beautiful drawing the way to draw I just drew it splashed it on actually at the time I was running out of ink and I was stuck with just one pen the drawing says it it's self dark and powerful it is saying you will not escape.

this is a dark and heroic piece the greatness of this piece of art in my eyes and to me it expresses love and power anger and frustration quite similar to other pieces it's class it flows like it is looking for a destination I painted it with energy.

This piece is a simple piece the country side and a bridge it looks like to me look at it twice it says what it says. I could never get my head around this piece as it is very unusual that I would normally draw something so normal.

This piece is an abstract piece some people say it is almost musical and flows with energy and look again you might change your mind. I could never get my mind around how I created it. the question is who is behind the door.

This piece is expected to look like what it actually is I did not know what I painted until the end this is not what I expected when I look at it, It reminds me of apartment blocks. I do not know how I painted it is a summer piece.

This particular piece is what it says it is one of my favourites it seems to say WEIRD, I find it striking.

This piece is one of my favourite it to me shows passion it is trippy and flows with character bright yellow reflecting the warmth of the sun. I found it like I was walking to the top of a mountain it was like I was at the top with one more step before I reached the very top of the giant mountain.

www.ingramcontent.com/pod-product-compliance
Lightning Source LLC
Chambersburg PA
CBHW030502220526
45464CB00006B/2613